FA

IT'S MUDDY OUT TODAY

Bil Keane

FAWCETT GOLD MEDAL • NEW YORK

A Fawcett Gold Medal Book
Published by Ballantine Books
Copyright © 1984 by Cowles Syndicate
Copyright © 1988 by King Features Syndicate, Inc.

Library of Congress Catalog Card Number: 88-91159

ISBN 0-449-13376-1

Manufactured in the United States of America

First Edition: December 1988

"It's startin' to rain, Mommy. Can we finish our game in the house?"

"Can we use the beach umbrella, Mommy? The sun is bad for our mud."

"You hafta shake your head both ways before you cross the street."

"I can't reach the brakes!"

"Know what, Mommy? I'm afraid your eyes are
bigger than my stomach."

"What do I hafta do to get one of those
BIG ones?"

"My wiggly tooth came out of its pocket!"

"Mommy! Why is your chicken wearing
leg warmers?"

"Miss Bunn thinks 'gross' means 12 dozen."

"Don't step on my toes, Daddy!"

"I'll eat your brownish stuff if you'll eat my
dark green stuff."

"But I don't WANT to belong to the clean plate club. I want to belong to the DIRTY plate club!"

"Typing is like tap-dancing with your fingers!"

"Mommy, this shirt has a leftover button."

"They can make us learn all this stuff now, but as soon as I'm old enough I'm gonna FORGET!"

"Mommy, would you take the bone out of my peach?"

"I CAN'T have my Daddy's nose. He's wearing it."

"I feel sorry for piggy banks. They look like
they've been stabbed."

"Daddy, will you pull out the cork?"

"I happen to be your mother and I do not wish to
be addressed as 'man.'"

"Mommy, did we get a piece of the cake you're eating in this picture?"

"Grandma, will you show me how to make a capital five?"

"Was St. Patrick married to Cleopatrick?"

"Try and find me, Mommy!"

"You repeat everything I say."
"I repeat everything you say?"

"Who are these people, Mommy? Looks like 'Clint Eastvooouund' and 'Merv Grifjiiimn' and. . . ."

"Well, can we have the soccer ball back if we play with it outside?"

"The right one is for cold, the left one's hot and the middle one's warm."

"Why is your dress falling off?"

"I'm collecting aluminum cans for recyclin',
Grandma. When yours are empty will
you mail them all to me?"

"Billy, I've told you a million times:
Don't exaggerate!"

"Listen, I'm going to hit a key."   "Now tell me which one it was."

"I feel sorry for Scrappy. He's an only dog."

"Mommy's gonna get some take-out money."

"I blew Daddy a kiss, but Dolly got in the way!"

"Just once I wish the bus would break down
GOING to school."

"In a minute it'll be channel three."

"Mommy! I can't hear Michael Jackson 'cause
Jeffy's gettin' in his way!"

"Mommy likes to hug Daddy 'cause she doesn't
have to bend over to do it."

"Playin' horsey is a NEAT idea, Daddy. Did you just make it up?"

"How can a book with no cartoons in it be
so funny, Mommy?"

"Ummm! This is a good recipe!"

"Daddy's gonna babysit himself."

"Was I born on a Monday, Mommy?"

"I'm grounded. I said one more word
to my mother."

"The Easter Bunny brings colored eggs, chocolates and ham."

"Mommy, are we gonna put lights on our
Easter lily?"

"What I don't like is when he gets up in his balcony and talks so long."

"Mommy! Billy says he's gonna check me into a Roach Motel!"

"I can't tell you what I have in my finger 'cause you'll try to take it out with a needle!"

"Out of the way, PJ! That's Barfy's favorite
dog food commercial!"

"That's a hibiscus."
"And is this one a low biscus?"

"Spiders sure waste a lot of thread."

"Sure I know where the pitchers warm up —
the ball pen."

"Can't I wear these again? All my stuff is
in the pockets."

"I wouldn't wanna be a flamingo. I'd hafta wear PINK all the time."

"Not me."

"Not me."

"Daddy said there'll always be prayer in school as
long as they give final exams."

"Adjust the color, Daddy. The man said Kentucky is bluegrass country and this looks green."

"We're playin' airplane."

"Daddy, who's your favorite little girl
who lives in this house?"

"You'll never get off the ground."

"You've got to eat some greens."
"Could I have a lime lollipop?"

"Mommy! Don't peek! We've got a surprise for tomorrow, but don't look! Mommy? . . ."

"You can say good, fine, nice, wonderful—lots of other things. 'Neat' isn't the only adjective in the English language."

"I'm NOT made of frogs and snails and
puppy-dogs' tails!"

"Daddy doesn't hit the ball over the net much, but he grunts just like Jimmy Connors."

"It's OK, Mommy. The yolk hit the pan. Only
the white part fell into the burner."

"That's because in baseball they don't blow
whistles all the time."

"But, Billy! Seven isn't old!"

"Mommy, can you energize me?"

"This time of the year school is just like TV.
Nothin' but reruns!"

"Don't tell me
it's going to
rain!"

"I won't
tell you,
Daddy."

"I can count to 10 and then back down again to 'blast-off.'"

"Our daddy's connectin' up our new
door chimes."

"They bring the picture closer, but
not the sound."

"Sticks and stones will break my bones, but names will never hurt me!"

"Mommy, could we get a penguin for a pet? We could keep the air conditioner on all year."

"That's the stern, and this is the bow."

"Daddy, do you have any touch-up paint
for the car?"

"It isn't break dancing. It's a tantrum!"

"He really has a long leash!"

"Martina's playin' Hana, and don't ask me their last names!"

"Oh, boy! It's gonna be like a bunch of Saturdays in a row!"

"I thought you came in here to get the children."

"Are Jacques Cousteau, Inspector Cousteau and
Robinson Cousteau brothers?"

"Look! It's raining up!"

"Know what's good about sign language? You can talk with your mouth full."

"Dolly says I won't be four till I get my
birthday cake."

"Mommy, tell me when my sunburn is done."

"If we're only gettin' daddy one present, who gets to give it to him?"

"Like it, Daddy? We had to go to three stores and one ice cream place before we bought it."

"No more break dancing!"

"HOT!"

"Lie still, Barfy. Think of it as a nice massage."

"Whoever cuts the grass is boss
of the family."

"I guess crickets only know that one tune."

"Daddy, there's something wrong with the nose wheel."

"Seven years I've spent learning to tie my shoelaces and NOW they give us Velcro."

"Cut it like Mr. T's."

"Cows give us milk and camels give us soup."

"Stop swimmin' so loud, Dolly! I can't
hear Mommy!"

"Daddy, will you come in the water with us
when you finish polishing Mommy?"

"I'm not goin' in again till the ocean stops wavin'."

"We're buildin' a golf course."

"How old do babies hafta get to start bein'
boys and girls?"

"OK, let her go."

"You can at least open your eyes, P.J.
Eyes can't hear."

"What was the name of that place where we saw the mules, Mommy?"

"The Grand Canyon!"

"It's OK, Aunt Nancy. You can have a lick 'cause you're FAMILY."

"Why don't we give the birds HOT water for their bath?"

"Guess what Kittycat's got in her mouth?"

"This time you be the hugs and I'll be the kisses."

"Why do you wear your bib on your lap, Grandma?"

"I hope the tooth fairy gives me a raise
with this one."

"What size batteries do lightning bugs take?"

"I never get to hear Michael Jackson in Grandma's car. The only station her radio can get is the 'Music of Your Life' one."

"I don't need the light on, Grandma. I don't
know how to read anyway!"

"I like the rain. It keeps my hair wet so I can comb it better."

"Mommy! Guess what I saw behind my
eyes last night."

"Echos are like talkin' to yourself in a mirror."

"No, Jeffy! It's not connected!"